Domby-Dom

A Play

"Denby Trubshaw"
(assisted by Nick Warburton)

A SAMUEL FRENCH ACTING EDITION

SAMUEL FRENCH

FOUNDED 1830

SAMUELFRENCH.COM
SAMUELFRENCH-LONDON.CO.UK

FOR PRODUCTION ENQUIRIES

UNITED STATES AND CANADA
Info@SamuelFrench.com
1-866-598-8449

UNITED KINGDOM AND EUROPE
Theatre@SamuelFrench-London.co.uk
020-7255-4302

Each title is subject to availability from Samuel French, depending upon country of performance. Please be aware that *DOMBY-DOM* may not be licensed by Samuel French in your territory. Professional and amateur producers should contact the nearest Samuel French office or licensing partner to verify availability.

MUSIC USE NOTE

Licensees are solely responsible for obtaining formal written permission from copyright owners to use copyrighted music in the performance of this play and are strongly cautioned to do so. If no such permission is obtained by the licensee, then the licensee must use only original music that the licensee owns and controls. Licensees are solely responsible and liable for all music clearances and shall indemnify the copyright owners of the play(s) and their licensing agent, Samuel French, against any costs, expenses, losses and liabilities arising from the use of music by licensees. Please contact the appropriate music licensing authority in your territory for the rights to any incidental music.

IMPORTANT BILLING AND CREDIT REQUIREMENTS

If you have obtained performance rights to this title, please refer to your licensing agreement for important billing and credit requirements.

CHARACTERS

Twenty-two children playing themselves and the following parts:

Teddy Smith
Jemima
Timmy
Popkins
Rats
Helpers

The action of the play takes place on a stage in a theatre

Time: the present

PRODUCTION NOTE

The play can be performed by almost any size of group
from about a dozen upwards. The parts are numbered
one to twenty-two, but many of them can be divided up
to increase the opportunities for speaking, or merged if
fewer actors are available. However, it is probably best
if the following actors play these roles:

> Four - the organizer
> Six - Teddy Smith
> Seven - Jemima
> Eleven and Twelve - set builders
> Thirteen - the scene changer
> Fourteen - Timmy
> Fifteen - Popkins

When the play within the play starts, the action is carried
out by the toys, with the actors making them move and
providing the voices. Contemporary references can be
changed at the whim of the cast and producers.

**Other plays by Nick Warburton
published by Samuel French Ltd:**

DOMBY-DOM

Music. The Lights come up on several large boxes

A group of children is surrounded by toys—teddies, dolls, cars, etc.—and is playing, unaware of the audience

One (*making the teddy walk*) Domby-domby-domby-dom. (*Making the teddy stop and knock at an imaginary door*) Knock-knock-knock. (*In a teddy voice*) Is there anyone in?

Two and Three make their toys walk to the door, while Four enters and watches

Two ⎤
Three ⎦ (*together*) Domby-domby-domby-dom.

Two (*in a toy voice*) Hallo. Who's there?
Three (*in a toy voice*) Hallo. Who's there?
One It's me. Teddy Smith. I've come round for tea.
Two You've come round for tea?
Three You've come round for tea?
One I've come round for tea.
Four (*crossly*) What *are* you doing?
One (*still as a teddy*) Oh, hallo. We're doing what you said, aren't we?
Two Yes, we're doing what you said.
Three Yes, we're doing…
Four (*to the toys*) I'm not talking to you. (*To the children*) I'm talking to you.
One (*in teddy's voice*) Oh, dear. S/he wants to talk to you. (*In own voice*) S/he wants to talk to me? (*In teddy's voice, making the teddy nod*) Yes, s/he wants to…

Four Will you pack that in? What are you doing, you clodpoles?
Two (*in own voice*) We're playing.
Three That's what you said, isn't it? Play?
Four Not play. A play. Do a play. With actors and things.
One *A* play? Oh. (*To the teddy*) Dearie me, we got it wrong.
Two Dearie, dearie, dearie me.
Four Stop that!

They make the toys cry

Stop it. Now. You're wasting time. Don't you realize? I said we'd do a play. Put on a play. And here you are, mucking about with a bunch of toys. It's ridiculous. (*Beat*) They aren't even in costume.
One (*in own voice*) Well, don't panic. We will do a play, if that's what you want.
Four It's not just what I want, mate. It's what I've told everyone we'd do. I said we'd put on a play. I did all the arrangements and you were going to do the play.
Three What arrangements?
Four For a start I asked all these people to come and see it.
One People? What people?
Four (*indicating the audience*) These people! Patiently waiting for something to happen.

The others peer at the audience. It's the first time they've noticed them

Three Oh dear.
Two Dearie me.
Four Exactly. So now what?

They make the toys wave

One (*in a teddy voice*) Hallo, everyone...
Four Don't keep doing that! We can't ask all these people to watch

half an hour of teddies waving and saying hallo! We have got to do a play!

Two But there's only [four] of us.

Four [Three] of you. I said I'd do the arrangements, that's all. You won't catch me appearing on stage.

Four exits in a huff

They watch him/her go

Three Dearie, dearie me.

One Well, we can't do a play on our own. I'd never remember the words.

Two I know. Let's ask them. (*Indicating the audience*) That's what they do in pantomimes, don't they?

Three They can't be in it. They've come to watch.

Two Well, we've got to do something. (*To the audience*) Listen, everyone: would you like to be in our play?

No response

Three Right, then. Just us.

Two But what are we going to do?

Three What else can we do? (*To the audience*) Ladies and genlemen, we present *Teddy Smith Comes to Tea*. (*Making the toy walk*) Domby-domby-domby-dom...

A voice calls from the audience

Six Oh no! Not again!

One Don't interrupt. (*Making the teddy walk*) Domby-domby-domby-dom...

Six comes on stage

Six *Teddy Smith Comes to Tea*? Are you serious? Look at these

people. Some of them have high-powered jobs. They don't want
to watch *Teddy Smith Comes to Tea*!
Two Well, we gave them the chance...
One But they couldn't be bothered.
Six Then you have to be a bit more forceful. (*To the audience*)
Right! Listen to me, you lot. Sit up and listen. Either some of you
get up and act, or you sit through thirty minutes of *Teddy Smith
Comes to Tea*. Now, what's it to be?

Pause

Several would-be actors flood on to the stage

There you are. Now all you have to do is get them acting.
Three Right... Well, what shall we do, then?
Five It's obvious, isn't it?

They all look at him/her

Teddy Smith Comes to Tea.

They continue to look at him/her

No, really. I mean, we can get to the heart of these characters.
Discover what makes them tick.
Seven Clockwork, mostly. Anyway, we haven't come up here to
do a play with Teddy blinking Smith.
One (*making the teddy cry*) I'm not good enough. Oh, dearie, dearie
me...
Two Now look what you've done. You've upset him.
One (*making the teddy walk off*) I'll just have to get back in my box
... and cry myself to sleep.
All Ahh!
Six No, no. Do stay. I'm sure we can find something for you to do.
Three But not have tea. That's too boring.
Five What, then?
Seven Well, what most people want is football.

Immediately there is a heated argument about this

Three No, no! I'd rather watch *Teddy Smith Comes to Tea.*
Seven Well, we could do *Teddy Sheringham Comes to Tea.*

More arguments break out

Eight No, what we want is space! The future! Science fiction!
One Well, make your minds up or at this rate it soon will be the future.
Seven What about football, then?
Nine No, no. We want an epic adventure. *Indiana Jones and the Temple of Doom.*
One Starring Teddy Smith.
Two *Indiana Jones and the Teddy of Doom.*
Seven Where's the football in that?
Three All right, then. *Indiana Sheringham and the Teddy of Doom.*
Eight But what about space?

A further heated argument, broken by...

Six Look, be quiet, all of you! We've been going about ten minutes and we haven't done a thing yet. We've got to get started.
One Started with what? We all want different things.
Six Then we'll put different things in it.
Seven Football!
Eight Space!
Nine Adventure!
One And Teddy Smith!
Six Yes, all of them. (*To the audience*) Ladies and gentlemen, we present—*Indiana Smith and the Cup Final of Doom*!
Eight Space, space, space!
Six Or—*The Return of the Tedi*! By ... who's it by?
Three No one. We're making it up as we go along.
Six We can't tell them that. They have to have a writer to talk about when it's over. With a proper writer's name.

Nine Denby Trubshaw!

Six Who?

Nine He's a writer.

Three Never heard of him.

Nine No, I just made him up.

Eight Well, I don't think much of Denby Trubshaw…

Six Look, there's no point arguing about his name. He doesn't even exist.

Two He does now. And anyway, they'll soon forget about the writer. They always do.

Three So—it's *Indiana Smith and the Cup Final of Doom*, or *The Return of the Tedi*, by Denby Trubshaw!

One Brilliant! Right, places, everyone! The story begins!

There is a bustle of activity and everyone gets ready to start. They arrange themselves on the boxes, leaving an acting space c. From now on, the scenes are created when the actors step into this space. When everyone is settled…

Good. Right…

But a group of set-helpers march on from the wings

What do you want?

Helper 1 We've been waiting back there to move the set.

Two What set?

Helper 2 Exactly. We've got nothing to do.

Helper 3 They said we had to help with the play…

Helper 1 Only you got it wrong. There wasn't a play.

Three Well, there is now.

Helper 2 Exactly. So we want to join in.

Five We can't have scene-shifters acting. Acting is specialised work.

Helper 1 (*threateningly*) We've got a settee and two armchairs out there, mush, and they're coming on *now* unless you let us act.

Two Oh, let them, for goodness' sake.

One All right, take your places.

The set-helpers take their places on the boxes

Ten Excuse me, but what about props and things?

Six There's always one awkward customer, isn't there?

Ten But we have to have a space station, and rockets and cars for a car chase...

Seven And a football pitch.

Two Well, funnily enough—we haven't got any of those things.

Three We could make them, I suppose.

Eleven I'll do that. I'm good with my hands.

One You'll have to be.

Six OK. Write this down. Two rockets, one football pitch...

Seven Wembley.

Eleven Wembley. I'm not sure I can manage that.

Seven Then do a scale model.

Eleven (*writing it down*) I'll see what I can manage.

Ten What about a helicopter?

Six Good idea, yes. Got that?

Eleven And a helicopter. Right. How long have I got?

Two About twelve minutes.

Eleven Time for a cup of tea first, then. But I'll need someone to help me.

Twelve I could lend a hand, but...

Eleven But what?

Twelve I don't like tea.

Eleven How about orange?

Twelve OK. Orange. I don't mind. What are we going to use to make all this?

Three The usual stuff. Egg boxes, washing-up liquid bottles. You've seen *Blue Peter*: you know the drill.

Eleven Fine. Off we go then.

Eleven and Twelve exit

Six And in the meantime, we'll have to make do with what we've got.

Five A bunch of toys.
Six They were a bunch of toys. Now they're actors.
One So... One day Teddy Smith was out for a jog...

Six makes the teddy jog

Six Domby-domby-dom...
Two When his faithful friend Jemima came screeching up...

Seven makes one of the toys screech up to the teddy, with a long, ear-splitting screech

...in a car.
Seven Oh. (*She grabs a car and repeats the noise. Then, in Jemima's voice*) Teddy Smith, Teddy Smith! Something terrible has happened!
Six What is it, Jemima!
Seven You know the Inter-Galaxy Cup Final is about to take place?
Six Of course. That's why I'm out jogging. I'm in training.
Nine In training? A teddy's going to play in the cup final? That's ridiculous.
Six It's all ridiculous, mate. Just keep going.
Nine But they'll never belive it.
Two They will if you do it fast enough. Keep going.
Seven Teddy Smith, Teddy Smith, a wicked villain has just sent us a postcard. He says he's going to destroy Wembley unless we pay him lots of money.
Six But that's terrible, Jemima. What's the name of this wicked villain?
Seven What?
Six What's his name?
Seven Oh, crikey.
Six O'Crikey. He's Irish, is he?
Seven No, I mean, oh, crikey, I haven't got to think of another name, have I?
Eight It's Timmy, Teddy Smith.
Ten Timmy? You can't have a villain called Timmy.

Eight Yes, you can. Timmy's a very villainous name.

Three Oh, well. Timmy it is, then. Press on.

Six We must act fast, Jemima. Let's get back to the flat and make some plans!

Eight So Teddy Smith and Jemima jumped in the car and drove off.

Seven makes the car drive round the stage. She keeps it going during the following

Nine Meanwhile, the evil genius ... Timmy ... was making his own plans.

Thirteen steps forward

Thirteen (*going all wobbly*) Blubbalubbalubba-lub!

The others watch for a moment

One What was that?

Thirteen That's what happens when you change scene. The screen goes all wobbly.

Three This is a stage, not a screen.

Thirteen I just thought it would be useful if I did the scene changes.

Three Blubbalubbalubba-lub?

Thirteen Well, why not?

One Oh, let him/her get on with it.

Thirteen repeats the sound—others may join in

Nine Where were we?

Three The evil genius...

Nine Oh, yes. Timmy. Meanwhile, Timmy was watching Teddy Smith on his multi-media water-resistant watch display panel. Who's Timmy?

Fourteen jumps about and puts her hand up. She looks a sweet little person

Fourteen Me, me, me!

Two You, an evil genius?

Fourteen Yes, please.

Two She looks too sweet to be evil.

Fourteen I'm not sweet. I'm quite naughty at times.

Five Naughty?

Fourteen Yes, the other day I absolutely refused to eat my fish-paste sandwiches.

Six Well, Timmy wants to take over the world and run it in his own cruel way. That's more than a bit naughty.

Fourteen Oh, go on. Let me be Timmy.

Two No.

Fourteen I'll be sick if you don't.

Two Too bad.

Fifteen No, I'm afraid she means she'll be sick. Actually sick. It's a threat.

Three She can't just be sick like that. Like turning on a tap.

Fourteen Oh, can't I? (*She winds herself up to be sick*)

One OK, OK, you're Timmy.

Fourteen Thank you very much. (*In a sweet voice*) Hah, hah! That nasty Teddy Smith thinks he can spoil my plans, does he? We'll see about that. Popkins!

Fifteen Yes, master?

One Who's Popkins?

Fourteen My evil assistant. I've got lots of evil assistants—Popkins and Wibbly and Blinkums…

One Just a minute. (*He does a quick count*) No, you've got one evil assistant. We're running out of actors.

Fourteen How can I take over the world with one measly evil assistant?

Three You'll have to do the best you can.

Fourteen Oh, well. Popkins!

Fifteen Yes, master.

Fourteen I'm going to crush that do-gooding, snivelly teddy bear once and for all! Ha-ha-ha!

Fifteen Yes, master. (*Beat*) That's all I say, is it? "Yes, master"?

Three We haven't got time for everyone to make long speeches.

Fifteen It's a bit boring for me, that's all—"Yes, master".
Fourteen Popkins?
Fifteen Yes, master?
Fourteen Do you want your feet roasted over a slow fire?
Fifteen No, master.
Fourteen Then get on with it.
One There you are. You've got another line now.
Fifteen What, "No, master"?
Fourteen Yes, Popkins. So don't moan. Call in the boys!
Fifteen Yes, master. (*He gestures to the wings*)

A troop of rats come on

Five They aren't boys; they're rats.
Fifteen They're in evil disguise.
Two No, this can't be right. I mean, they've just come on, dressed
as rats...
Eight Yes?
Two And they must've been waiting there—dressed as rats—since
we started.
Nine So?
Two So no-one's going to believe we're making this up as we go
along, are they? This has blown the illusion.
Eight Not necessarily. We could tell them we created the rats with
the power of our imaginations.
Two Oh, yes?
One Look, it doesn't matter what they believe. The rats are on and
that's that.
Fifteen Anyway, they're the audience. They believe what we tell
them to believe.
Two In that case, carry on, rats!

*The rats go into an evil dance to the music of "In the Hall of the
Mountain King" or similar. When they've finished...*

Three When they'd done their evil dance, the rats jumped into the
cars and Popkins sent them out...

Eight In the cars? Ordinary cars?
Fourteen What's wrong with that?
Eight Well, I haven't noticed much space in it so far.
Five I know. Popkins, send out the *flying* cars.
Eight Thank you.
Thirteen Hang on.

The scene-changing group go into action with cries of "Blubbalubbalubba-lub!" Several people hurtle round the stage with toy cars, making car noises

Six Jemima, I think we're being followed.
Seven (*looking back*) Good grief! Flying cars!
Six I thought as much. Step on it, Jemima!
Seven Right-oh! (*She grabs one of the cars and steps on it*)
Sixteen What did you do that for?
Seven Teddy Smith told me to.
Sixteen You've bent it. I'll get you for that.
Seven You'll have to catch me first.

Teddy and Jemima hare off again. A car chase follows. They come to the front and stop. Their pursuers stop too, a little way behind. They make sounds of engines idling

Six Jemima?
Seven Yes, Teddy Smith?
Six When I said step on it, I meant step on the speed.
Seven Oh, I see. Sorry.

They hare off again and the others follow

One (*watching*) This is good stuff, this is.
Three Yes. Very exciting.
Two Nice cars.
Five Very lifelike.
Ten Excuse me.

One Now what?

Ten Just stop running around a moment, will you?

The car chase stops and they make more idling noises

Thank you. They might be nice cars, but nobody can actually see them. Not properly.

Five What do you mean? I can see them.

Ten But the audience can't. I think you should show them. In close-up.

Thirteen Right, team! Close-up! Blubbalubbalubba-lub!

Two We can't do close-ups, you fool. We're on stage.

Thirteen Sorry, sorry.

Ten No, you'll just have to send a couple of cars down into the audience. So they can see the detail.

Nine That's a good idea. Grab a couple of cars and show that lot down there.

Eight Right, on with the chase!

Some of the rats take their cars into the audience to show them round. They continue doing this as the chase proceeds on stage. The others watch for a while. Then...

Five How long is this going on? I mean, it's very good, but how does it end?

Sixteen We don't know. No-one's told us.

Two Teddy Smith had better fight them off.

Six Right.

The cars screech to a halt and blows are exchanged

Sixteen It's no good. We're outnumbered!

Eighteen How can we be outnumbered? There's only two of them.

Sixteen Hey, that's right. Hang on a minute.

The fight stops and the rats go to the front of the stage and call to their companions

Hoy! You [two]! What do you think you're doing?

Nineteen *(from the audience)* We're showing the cars to the audience.

Eighteen Get back up here!

Nineteen Well, he says he wants to swap it for his belt...

Eighteen Get back up here now! We're in the middle of a fight.

Nineteen Sorry, sorry.

The rats in the audience return to the stage and the fight starts again. The others watch for a while

Seventeen Very good fight. Very realistic.

Three Very.

One They look as if they really mean it.

It becomes apparent that the fight is real. The fighters are rolling all over the place

Two They do mean it! Hey! Break it up, you lot!

Sixteen Well, she trod on my car.

One I'm sure she didn't mean it.

Seven Oh, yes, I did.

The fight breaks out again and has to be stopped

Nine Pack it in! *(To Thirteen)* You! Change scene quickly!

Thirteen Blubbalubbalubba-lub!

The fighters retire, rather groggily

Two So, where are we now?

Seven Wembley. Then we need the set. *(She calls off)* Oi!

Twelve appears, covered in paint and wearing an apron

Twelve What?

Five Have you finished the set yet?

Twelve Nearly. We've just got the roof and the helicopters to do.

Two Forget the helicopters. We need Wembley now.

Twelve Wembley wasn't built in a day, you know. Talk among yourselves. We'll be with you in a minute.

Twelve exits

Two (*to Timmy*) You'd better get on with it, then.

Fourteen OK. (*With an evil laugh, followed by a sweet voice*) Hah-hah, Popkins! Here we are at Wembley.

Nine Not quite. You're still on your way. Make something up.

Fourteen Ah hah! ...It's a beautiful day, Popkins.

Fifteen Yes, master.

Fourteen A beautiful day for destroying the heart of English football! Hah-hah!

Fifteen Yes, master.

Pause. They look around uncertainly

Fourteen I don't suppose you've seen Wembley yet, have you, Popkins?

Fifteen No, master.

Fourteen Oh. (*Beat*) Pity.

Pause. They all look off

Twelve (*off; calling*) Nearly ready.

One of the rats comes forward

Rat We could do our rat dance again, if you like.

Eight (*briefly*) No, thank you. (*Coming forward*) Perhaps this would be a good time to point out that today's the day that England play Outer Galactos in the Inter Galaxy Cup Final.

Three Good idea, yes. Let's get the experts in to talk about it.

Three football pundits come forward with chairs

Twenty Tough game for England, don't you think, Jimmy?

Twenty-one Very tough, Des. They're a strong team, Outer Galactos. And very experienced. Their average age is a hundred and forty and that's a lot of experience, Des.

Twenty Can England do it, do you think, Trevor?

Twenty-two Well, Des, I don't know. But it's goin' to be fascinatin' to see them battlin' against those poundin' twenty-six legs of the Galactos lads.

Twenty Quite, Jimmy, all those legs will give the alien strikers a bit of an advantage in the box. What can England do about that?

Twenty-one Well, Des, if I was Glyn Doddle, I'd tell the lads to keep the ball in the air. They don't head a ball very well on Outer Galactos.

Twenty Quite. Not having any heads to head with. Well, I can see Wembley looking splendid in the April sunshine...

Twelve (*off*) No, you can't.

Twenty ...but before we start, let's just go over for the Outer Galactos national anthem.

Thirteen Blubbalubbalubba-lub!

A group gathers with hands on hearts and heads tucked inside their tops

Group (*singing*) Bing-bong! Bing-bing-bong!

The group retires

Twenty-two Doesn't take them long, Des, singin' their anthem, does it?

Twenty No, Trevor. Let's hope the game's a bit more lively.

Twenty-two A bit more int'restin', yes, Des.

Twenty Well ... any more thoughts, Jimmy?

Twenty-one Not really, Des, no.

Twelve (*off*) Nearly ready.

The pundits retire with relief. The following scene changes take place quickly

Five Meanwhile, Teddy Smith and Jemima were hurrying to Wembley, too.

Thirteen Blubbalubbalubba-lub!

Six   ⎰ *(together; making the toys run)* Domby-domby-domby-
Seven   ⎱ dom!

One As they got nearer, so did Timmy and Popkins...

Thirteen Blubbalubbalubba-lub!

Fourteen Faster, Popkins! Faster!

Fifteen Domby-domby-domby-dom, master!

Three Nearer and nearer...

Two Teddy Smith and Jemima...

Thirteen Blubbalubbalubba-lub!

Six Faster, Jemima! Faster!

Seven Domby-domby-domby-dom!

Three Nearer and nearer...

While the scenes change and the toys run, Twelve appears and gives a thumbs up sign

Ten Suddenly, Wembley came into view!

Eleven and Twelve come on with a model of a football stadium. They look worn out

The others gather round to admire it

Five Oh, well done. Lovely detail.

Timmy and Popkins hurtle up

Fourteen We've arrived, Popkins! We got here first!

Fifteen Yes, master.

Fourteen Have they paid over the money, Popkins?

Fifteen No, master.

Fourteen Then Wembley must be destroyed! (*She stamps on the model*)

There is a stunned silence

Eleven (*quietly and slowly*) You berk.

Fourteen Why? I said I would destroy Wembley.

Twelve We've only just made the blinking thing. The paint's still wet.

Fourteen I can't help that. I'm evil.

Teddy and Jemima hurtle up

Seven Oh, Teddy Smith! We're too late.

Eleven You certainly are, you pair of wallies.

Six Not so, Jemima. You might think we're too late, but you're forgetting my secret watch.

Seven Am I?

Six It has a reverse-time re-do button, remember?

Seven If you say so.

One But of course! Teddy Smith is actually just in time. If he presses the button on his watch, Wembley will be restored to its former glory.

Ten That's a bit far-fetched, isn't it?

Nine No, no. I believe James Bond has a watch like that. It makes sense.

Seven Then don't just stand there, Teddy Smith! Press the blinking button!

Fourteen Oh, no, you don't! Popkins, grab that watch!

There is a fierce struggle. Suddenly Popkins grabs the toy Teddy Smith and breaks free. They all freeze

Fifteen Hand over the money or the bear gets it!

All Never!

Fifteen Right! (*He drop-kicks the teddy into the audience*)

Six goes chasing after it

Fourteen You fool, Popkins!
Fifteen Now what?
Fourteen He's still got the watch!
Three Teddy Smith was knocked clear of the fray, and that meant he was free to press the button on the watch.
Fifteen Oh, I see. Sorry, master.
Six (*having retrieved Teddy Smith*) I'm pressing the button now!

They all cringe. Nothing happens

One So now what happens?
Five Well, the button's been pressed so Wembley is restored.
All Flash!
Two (*to Eleven and Twelve*) We need another Wembley, I'm afraid.
Eleven You what?
Three That's how the story ends. Wembley is restored. Suddenly.
Two In an instant.
Eleven You must be joking.
One Don't blame us, blame Denby Trubshaw.
Eleven (*throwing down his/her apron and stalking off*) In your dreams, mate. I'm going on strike.

Eleven exits

Three So now what?
Twelve No need to worry. Just wait there.

Twelve goes off and returns with another model

Here's one I made earlier.
Five Then the game can go ahead.

All Hooray!

Five So that is the end of *Teddy Smith and the Cup Final of Doom...*

Three Or *The Return of the Tedi.*

Two Wembley was destroyed by the evil Timmy...

Nine One-nil to the baddies.

One But restored by the brave and resourceful Teddy Smith.

Eight One-all!

Ten Actually, one-all means it's a draw.

Seven That's true. We need a penalty shoot-out.

Sixteen Oh, no, not that!

Seven It's the fairest way.

Eighteen Oh, no, it isn't.

Others Oh, yes, it is!

A heated argument follows

   Four enters and blows a whistle

The argument stops

Four Time! Everybody off!

Seven But what about the penalty shoot-out?

Five And what about the match?

Four If you think we're staging a football match with six-legged, headless aliens, you're very much mistaken. That is the end of the play.

All groan with disappointment

   Well, I must say I'm surprised. You managed to put on a whole play, starting from nothing. It was a complete load of rubbish, but you managed to do it. So. Get clearing up. There's paint and glue all over the shop out there. Come on. Get moving! (*S/he blows the whistle*)

   They all go off talking. Everything is removed, except Teddy

Smith. Then Six comes on again and picks Teddy Smith up. S/he makes him walk off as the Lights dim and the music comes up

Six Domby-domby-domby-dom…

CURTAIN

FURNITURE AND PROPERTY LIST

Further dressing may be added at the director's discretion

On stage: Large boxes
Toys: teddies, dolls, cars, etc.

Off stage: Model of Wembley (**Eleven** and **Twelve**)
Model of Wembley (**Eleven** and **Twelve**)

Personal: **Eleven:** notepad, pen
Seven: wrist-watch
Four: whistle

LIGHTING PLOT

Property fittings required: nil
Interior. The same throughout

To open: Overall general lighting

Cue 1   **Six** makes teddy walk off   (Page 21)
            Fade lights

EFFECTS PLOT

Cue 1   To open   (Page 1)
Music

Cue 2   **Two**: "In that case, carry on, rats!"   (Page 11)
Music: In the Hall of the Mountain King *or similar,*
   cut when ready

Cue 3   **Six** makes teddy walk off   (Page 21)
Music